Presented To:

Presented By:

Date:

From a
Grandmother's
Heart

NELSON BOOKS
A Division of Thomas Nelson Publishers
Since 1798

www.thomasnelson.com

Published in Nashville, Tennessee, by Thomas Nelson, Inc.

Nelson Books titles may be purchased in bulk for educational, business, fund-raising, or sales promotional use. For information, please e-mail SpecialMarkets@ThomasNelson.com.

Managing Editor: Lila Empson
Associate Editor: Kyle L. Olund
Manuscript: Sheila Rabe
Design: Whisner Design Group, Tulsa, Oklahoma

Library of Congress Cataloging-in-Publication Data

From a grandmother's heart : 50 reflections on living well for my grandchild.
   p. cm.
 ISBN 0-7852-1480-1 (hardcover)
 1. Christian children--Prayer-books and devotions--English. 2. Grandchildren--Prayer-books and devotions--English. 3. Christian life--Juvenile literature.
 BV4870.F86 2005
 248.4--dc22

2005028179
Printed in the United States of America

06 07 08 09 QW 5 4 3 2 1

*Try to do to others as you would have them do to you,
and do not be discouraged if they fail sometimes.*

Charles Dickens

Contents

Introduction 9

1. The arrival of a grandchild is a life-changing event 10

2. God can help you accomplish anything you can dream,
   and even more 12

3. It's okay to be different, because God made you unique 14

4. Now is the perfect time to think about lifetime habits 16

5. When you stand up to a bully, you save his future
   victims as well as yourself 18

6. The best friends are the ones who aren't afraid to stop
   you from messing up 20

7. Everything you need to know to make your life good,
   you'll find in the Bible 24

8. It's great to go along with the crowd as long as they're
   only going out for pizza 26

9. Your biggest triumphs can grow out of your most
   miserable experiences 28

10. It's fun to be popular, but it's important to have good character ... 30

11. The best way to improve yourself is from the inside out 32

12. The secret to making your life easier is to always tell the truth ... 34

13. The only way to make chores disappear is to do them 38

14. It's always smart to think before you speak, especially
    when you're mad 40

15. When you maintain your body, you're caring for a precious
    piece of equipment 42

16. If you put yourself in other people's shoes, you won't
    step on their toes 44

17. The best people to hang out with are the ones who
    bring out your best 46

18. You can show your parents you love them by respecting them 48

19. Getting what you want in life starts with a wish but ends
    with an action 52

20. A problem is really a call to adventure 54

21. A feeling of accomplishment always makes up for the
    work it required 56

22. Tomorrow's happiest memories can be the things you do
    with your family today 58

23. If you have fun playing the game, it won't matter if you win or lose 60

24. Life is more exciting when you're open to trying new things 62

25. Like a muscle, talent gets bigger the more you exercise it 66

26. You can share everything with God because He will listen
to anything you have to say 68

27. The best way to appreciate your life is to think about all
the good in it 70

28. "I'm sorry" are the two most powerful words in the English language   72

29. In all aspects of life, the most important person to compete
against is yourself 74

30. The best way to gain trust is to show responsibility 76

31. The way you win in life is by playing by God's rules 78

32. It's always wiser to talk to people than about people 82

33. The way to keep friends is to look at your own faults
and ignore theirs 84

34. A failure is just a stubbed toe on the road to success 86

35. It's always a good idea to let someone else do
your bragging for you 88

36. Follow the law, and you'll detour around a lot of trouble 90

37. You can always make a bad day better by doing something
nice for someone else 92

38. Working together is the best way to conquer big jobs 96

39. God is strong enough to carry you through any mess 98

40. Leave your hurts in the past so that your present
and future can be better 100

41. What you do with the money you have is what makes you rich 102

42. The secret to succeeding is to keep trying 104

43. The best advice always comes from the people who care the most 106

44. Wise choices make for good living 110

45. Helping someone in need is like giving a gift to God 112

46. The biggest thrills are the ones that build character 114

47. Before you do anything, always remind yourself
that God sees everything 116

48. One of the most important things you can give God is your youth 118

49. Be a lifelong learner, and your life will always be interesting 120

50. God is the world's best guidance counselor, so trust
Him to guide your life 122

Introduction

In case you haven't guessed, this grandparent
thinks you're great. Watching you learn and
succeed at new things is always an adventure.
Spending time with you is a joy and a privi-
lege, and I love being able to share with you
some of the things I've learned in my life. I
know you'll apply them wisely to your own.
Your youthful energy and enthusiasm amaze
and delight me.

It's exciting to watch you develop your interests and hobbies and pursue your goals with
such zeal and determination. I see so much
potential in you, and that excites me. I can
hardly wait to see what you'll do with your life.
Whatever you do, I know you'll make your
family proud.

> Use your gifts
> faithfully, and they
> shall be enlarged;
> practice what you
> know, and you
> shall attain to
> higher knowledge.
>
> Matthew Arnold

Do not neglect the gift that is in you . . . Put these things into
practice, devote yourself to them, so that all may see your progress.

1 Timothy 4:14–15 NRSV

*The arrival of a grandchild
is a life-changing event.*

*Your presence in the world
makes life special for me.*

When you arrived, lots of people got excited: your parents, of course, and other family members. But the person who got most excited was me. This is because you are big stuff in a grandparent's life, the child of my child, which makes you doubly precious. You give my life new meaning. You are the good old days made new. You are the future. You are hugs and laughter and old board games brought out of the cupboard and dusted off. To hear from you makes me smile, and to spend time with you makes my day. Your presence in my life is my consolation for getting old and my reminder of why it's good to be alive. You make life fun!

Perfect love sometimes does not come until the first grandchild.

Welsh Proverb

Children are a gift from the LORD; they are a reward from him.

Psalm 127:3 NLT

God can help you accomplish anything you can dream, and even more.

God puts dreams in people's hearts, so trust Him to make yours come true.

Congratulations. You have reached the perfect time of life for big dreams. You not only have God-given gifts, but you also have the youth and energy to develop and use those gifts. The future is still an untapped resource just waiting to be used by you. Let your imagination carry you from possibility to fully formed idea. Soar mentally. Do you see yourself as the Columbus of space exploration, ready to discover a new planet, or a modern-day Marie Curie of research, who will find the cure for cancer? Will you write a best seller? Create a new technology? Perhaps you'll become a professor or a brain surgeon. Who knows? Dream that dream, and let God help you make it a reality.

No dreamer is ever too small; no dream is ever too big.

Author Unknown

To him who is able to do immeasurably more than all we ask or imagine, according to his power that is at work within us, to him be glory in the church and in Christ Jesus throughout all generations, for ever and ever! Amen.

Ephesians 3:20–21 NIV

*It's okay to be different,
because God made you unique.*

Be yourself, and your life will be good.

When you're young, being different can feel like the kiss of death. But things have a way of shifting as people get older, and the person who was once misunderstood or called cruel names often winds up being admired and called new names, like *genius* or *boss* (as in, "Yes, Boss, I'll get that coffee for you right away"). Resist the temptation to worry about what people will think if you dare to be different. Instead, concentrate on what God thinks about you. Please God by developing the talents He gave you. Do that and you'll find plenty of friends along the way, because ultimately everyone who is anyone appreciates people who are brave enough to be true to themselves.

If God accepts me as I am, then I had better do the same.

Hugh Montefiore

I praise you because you made me in an amazing and wonderful way. What you have done is wonderful. I know this very well.

Psalm 139:14 NCV

15

Now is the perfect time to think about lifetime habits.

Never put off till tomorrow habits that can make your life better starting today.

Habits are a little like people. Some are big, some are small, some are good, some are irritating, and some you'll want to avoid. Those undesirable ones can become your buddy in a heartbeat and then insist on sticking to you like superglue. Good ones may be a little harder to cultivate, but once you cultivate them, they'll be your friend for life and introduce you to all kinds of good things: health, achievement, and confidence. Now, while you're young, my grandchild, is the perfect time to develop the kind of habits that will make your life good. This is the time to get smart about how you spend your time and your money, about what you put into your mouth and your mind. Make friends with good habits, and you'll thank yourself later.

> We first make our habits, then our habits make us.
>
> John Dryden

Be very careful, then, how you live—not as unwise but as wise.

Ephesians 5:15 NIV

When you stand up to a bully, you save his future victims as well as yourself.

You'll feel better about yourself and make your life better when you stand up to bullies.

Bullies and weeds have a lot in common. They both pop up where they're least wanted and try to take over. A bully's strength depends on the fear of others. Intimidation is the game. When you stand up to a bully, you change the game rules and remove his advantage. A bully may try to push you, but remember that bullies won't push for long against a cement wall. They only want to push what will easily fall over. When you won't fall, the bully will give up pushing. Bullies fear and respect courage. They understand that it's useless to try to intimidate a person brave enough to look past their tough facade. And once you reveal that toughness as a facade, the bully is out of business. No one is buying his line.

> Courage faces fear and thereby masters it.
>
> Martin Luther King Jr.

Speak up for those who cannot speak for themselves; defend the rights of all those who have nothing.

Proverbs 31:8 NCV

The best friends are the ones who aren't afraid to stop you from messing up.

Be thankful for the honest friends God puts in your life, because they are the ones who are really there for you.

Everyone should have at least one friend who has a good head on his shoulders. Not the kind of friend who refuses to cut loose and have fun, but the kind who can tell a good time from a bad idea, the kind who will say, "Are you nuts? You can't do that." You'll never have a hard time finding friends to laugh with or to come to your house and inhale the last potato chip out of the pantry. But you might have trouble finding ones who really care enough to gently tell you when you're in danger of making a bad choice. The friend who will risk your anger to tell you an unpleasant truth or risk your friendship to save your life is the truest friend you can ever find.

A true friend never gets in your way unless you happen to be going down.

Arnold H. Glasgow

A friend loves at all times, and is born, as is a brother, for adversity.

Proverbs 17:17 AMP

Please God by developing the
talents He gave you.

You not only have God-given gifts, but
you also have the youth and energy to
develop and use those gifts.

You are the future.

Everything you need to know to make your life good, you'll find in the Bible.

Make a habit of reading your Bible now when you're young, and you'll reap the benefits your whole life.

Want to know how to win friends and influence people, how to avoid poor decisions? Want to learn how to face challenges, manage money, live an inspired life? How would you like to learn from somebody else's mistakes rather than your own? You could go out and buy a truckload of self-help books and hope that some of them actually help, or you could cover all that territory effectively with just one book: the Bible. The Bible has it all: wise advice, inspiring stories, truth, and God's blueprint for a meaningful life. You'll find everything you need between the covers of the Bible, and the more you read and apply what you read, the better your life will be.

> The existence of the Bible, as a book for the people, is the greatest benefit which the human race has ever experienced.
>
> Immanuel Kant

All scripture is inspired by God and is useful for teaching,
for reproof, for correction, and for training in righteousness,
so that everyone who belongs to God may be
proficient, equipped for every good work.

2 Timothy 3:16–17 NRSV

It's great to go along with the crowd as long as they're only going out for pizza.

Never let other people pressure you into doing something that doesn't feel right.

There's just something about hanging with the gang, isn't there? I know how in my past, going places with other people guaranteed laughs and a good time. But if someone gets an inspiration to do something that spells trouble, going along with the gang will guarantee that you'll learn the definition of *trouble* as well as how to spell it. Even if you don't actually participate in the behavior, you can end up caught in the fallout. You'll keep your life free of unnecessary unhappiness if you learn to discern when it's good to go along with the crowd and when it's better to say, "See you later," and let them move on without you. If going along ever looks easier, remember that standing up and stepping away from trouble will feel better.

> Only dead fish go with the current.
>
> Author Unknown

The wise see danger ahead and avoid it,
but fools keep going and get into trouble.

Proverbs 27:12 NCV

Your biggest triumphs can grow out of your most miserable experiences.

Don't get discouraged by unpleasant or unhappy experiences—God is still working on your behalf.

Some of the greatest songs have been written under the influence of a broken heart. Some of the greatest poetry has grown out of great misery. Fame has often come from sacrifice, and glory from death. Christ Himself had to endure death before the triumph of resurrection. God can always bring good out of even your worst experiences. Some of the toughest times in my life turned out to be the foundation for something important, something great. You, too, can come out of life's fires shining like gold if you let God guide you to the right fire exit. If you keep your eyes open, you may be able to see God at work in those miserable experiences. You may see Him turning you into something even more special than you already are.

> All our difficulties are only platforms for the manifestation of His grace, power, and love.
>
> Hudson Taylor

We are assured and know that [God being a partner in their labor] all things work together and are [fitting into a plan] for good to and for those who love God and are called according to [His] design and purpose.

Romans 8:28 AMP

It's fun to be popular, but it's important to have good character.

Having good character is more important than having friends.

Who doesn't like to be popular? After all, it's great to have lots of friends to hang out with, to laugh with, and to share adventures. But never sacrifice character to popularity. Popularity guarantees other people will want to be with you, but character guarantees you'll want to be with yourself. Popularity can rest on selfishness. A person may become popular simply for having something others want: a fun house to hang at, social prestige, money, good times. Character draws people for entirely different reasons: respect, admiration, trust. Friends are great. I've had many friends over the years, and I still like making new ones. Collect lots of friends yourself. But never give up your good character to get a friend.

> Happiness is not the end of life; character is.
>
> Henry Ward Beecher

A single day in your courts is better than a thousand anywhere else!
I would rather be a gatekeeper in the house of my God than
live the good life in the homes of the wicked.

Psalm 84:10 NLT

The best way to improve yourself is from the inside out.

Always be your fabulous self on the inside and remember that your outside appearance is only frosting on the cake.

Makeovers are the hot new thing. It can be
exciting to get fit and get a new look, but
don't forget that the most important makeover
of all is the one that takes place on the inside.
You are more than your face and your body
and the clothes you climb into every day.
Looking good on the outside will take you only
so far in life, especially at the rate fashion
changes. The look that really counts is the look
in your eyes when you meet new people or
see a need. Of course, you'll always want to
look your best, but the most important part of
yourself to keep improving will always be your
heart. Don't depend on fashion too much,
because it changes all the time—just look
through family photos to see some of the
goofy clothing and hairstyles I had over the
years.

Pretty is as pretty
does; handsome
is as handsome
does.

Author Unknown

Create in me a pure heart, O God,
and renew a steadfast spirit within me.

Psalm 51:10 NIV

33

The secret to making your life easier is to always tell the truth.

Telling the truth is always the best way to solve life's problems. And that's no lie.

When faced with a choice between the truth and a lie, grandchild, choose truth. Lying brings bad consequences. Lies are harder to hide than a pet elephant, and they attract problems like a magnet attracts metal shavings. Fibs, stretching the truth, deception—no matter what you call them, they hurt others and dig you into a mess. In my life I've discovered that lies lead to bigger lies that make problems worse and make you feel worse. Telling the truth, even when you've done something wrong, is liberating. It clears your conscience and your mind, and it stops that slippery slide to disaster, which happens the moment you lie. Life can get complicated, but being truthful will simplify much of it. So if you want to avoid a lot of unhappiness, tell the truth.

> Truth has no special time of its own. Its hour is now—always.
>
> Albert Schweitzer

Truth stands the test of time; lies are soon exposed.

Proverbs 12:19 NLT

Learn to discern when it's good to
go along with the crowd and when
it's better to say, "See you later."

You can come out of life's fires
shining like gold if you let God
guide you to the right fire exit.

You'll find everything you need
between the covers of the Bible.

The only way to make chores disappear is to do them.

The sooner you dig in and do a chore, the sooner you're free to do the things you really want to do.

Chores—they can be boring, they often involve hard work, and they usually want to take you away from something fun. They never go away—even grandmothers like me still have to do them—they never say, "Well, I can see you're busy with something way cool right now, so don't worry. I'll just take care of myself." In spite of their high irritation factor, chores are important. They make things happen. Chores make stinky garbage disappear from the house and make sure much-loved pets don't go hungry. They teach diligence and responsibility, and they reward you with satisfaction when completed. Next time you're faced with a chore, try to think of it as if you're eating vegetables—not always exciting but very good for you. And the best way to get them off your plate is to dig in.

Having once decided to achieve a certain task, achieve it at all costs of tedium and distaste. The gain in self-confidence of having accomplished a tiresome labor is immense.

Thomas Arnold Bennett

The diligent find freedom in their work;
the lazy are oppressed by work.

Proverbs 12:24 MSG

It's always smart to think before you speak, especially when you're mad.

Making a habit of thinking before you speak will save you much embarrassment and grief, and it will preserve many friendships.

When it comes to words, people often forget the brilliant things you say. But say something not so smart, and they'll store it in their memory banks forever. That's why, as I've learned from firsthand experience, it's always good to audition your words before you let them loose in public. Install a brain-to-mouth filter in your mind that checks your thoughts before they can turn verbal and make trouble. In other words, think before you speak. Ask yourself, "If I say this, will I make the situation better or worse? Will I be sorry later?" If the answers are yes, shut your lips and imprison those words. Never let anger propel your words into a situation where they can explode a relationship. You're a smart grandchild, and you prove it every time you think before you speak.

> If I raise my voice, may it be only in praises.
>
> Max Lucado

Post this at all intersections, dear friends: Lead with your ears, follow up with your tongue, and let anger straggle along in the rear.

James 1:19 MSG

When you maintain your body, you're caring for a precious piece of equipment.

You only get one body in this life, so treat it well.

Your body is the human equivalent of a Ferrari—ultravaluable! Fueled by all your youthful energy, it will get you around faster than I can even think of moving. Your body allows you to express happiness, jump around at concerts, and then enjoy a great hamburger afterward. It is your finely tooled piece of equipment for both work and play. And that's why it's a very good idea to maintain that body. Exercise it. Like a fine car, it needs to be driven. It also needs the right kind of fuel so it can race well, so fuel it with good, healthful food. (Too many post-concert hamburgers will clog your carburetor.) Maintain that precious body of yours, and it will serve you well for a lifetime.

Ill health, of body or mind, is defeat. Health alone is victory. Let all men, if they can manage it, contrive to be healthy.

Thomas Carlyle

You should know that your body is a temple
for the Holy Spirit who is in you.

1 Corinthians 6:19 NCV

If you put yourself in other people's shoes, you won't step on their toes.

You can't go wrong in life by considering the feelings of others.

It's an awful thing, isn't it, when someone says or does something thoughtless or mean to you? It hurts, and when that happens you have to wonder what that person was thinking. Don't waste time wondering, because the answer is simple. That person wasn't thinking, at least not about you.

You don't want to make other people uncomfortable or unhappy like that, so before you say or do anything, always put yourself in the other person's tennis shoes. Ask yourself how you would want to be treated. Answer honestly and then act accordingly. That's called the Golden Rule, and if you live by it you will always treat others fairly. And here's a bonus—other people will probably treat you better too.

Try to do to others as you would have them do to you, and do not be discouraged if they fail sometimes.

Charles Dickens

Do to others as you would have them do to you.

Luke 6:31 NRSV

The best people to hang out with are the ones who bring out your best.

Because the friends you pick will be an important part of your life, pick them carefully.

People—the world is full of them—fun people, silly people, serious people, talented people, overachievers, underachievers, movers and shakers, and troublemakers. That leaves a lot of options when you're picking friends. As you explore your options, remember that you're choosing more than just a friend; you're choosing interests and attitudes to share and a lifestyle to adopt, because friends hang together. Friends can influence one another for good or bad. *Peer pressure* isn't just a term some sociologist made up; it's a fact of life. With the wrong friends, it can be an unpleasant fact. Of course, you'll want to pick peers who pressure you to be your best possible self, who encourage you to dream big and aim high. Hang with that kind of gang, and you're sure to soar.

Bad company is a disease; who lies with dogs will rise with fleas.

Rowland Watkyns

Whoever walks with the wise will become wise;
whoever walks with fools will suffer harm.

Proverbs 13:20 NLT

You can show your parents you love them by respecting them.

Always remember that your parents love you, and try to treat them with respect.

Parents are ordinary people who, once they have a child, must acquire extraordinary wisdom and endurance. Being a parent is a job for Superman and Wonder Woman, but your parents do the best they can without the advantage of superhero powers. Now, that's bravery! It's also love. You are the biggest, best, most special thing in your parents' lives, and they love you like nothing else. You love them, too. So how to show it? Of course, parents enjoy gifts and appreciate *I love you*'s. But what most shows a parent your love is respect. When you speak respectfully to your parents and try hard to obey their rules, you're showing them in a tangible way that you love them and that they matter. Words are great, but respect speaks louder.

> Honor your parents both in your thoughts and speech and behavior.
>
> Richard Baxter

Honor (esteem and value as precious) your father and your mother— this is the first commandment with a promise.

Ephesians 6:2 AMP

Before you say or do anything, always put yourself in the other person's tennis shoes.

Words are great, but respect speaks louder.

Never let anger propel your words into a situation where they can explode a relationship.

Getting what you want in life starts with a wish but ends with an action.

The surest way to make a dream a reality is to plan for it, trust God to help you achieve it, and then work for it.

Ever hear the saying, "You've got to have a dream before you can have a dream come true"? That's certainly where it all begins, with a hope in your heart. But that's not where it ends. Having a dream is like opening a map and finding the place where you want to go. It's a very important step, but it's only a first step. Many people open the map but never get beyond looking at it. In the end, this won't take them far. The secret is to have a plan as well as a destination. You can reach your dreams if you make your travel arrangements and then take the necessary steps to get there. You'll be surprised how many dreams you can make come true this way.

A dream is just a dream. A goal is a dream with a plan and a deadline.

Harvey MacKay

All hard work brings a profit, but mere talk leads only to poverty.

Proverbs 14:23 NIV

A problem is really a call to adventure.

You'll be able to face problems better if you see them as a door to adventure rather than as a wall stopping you.

Some people look at a problem and fail to see its potential. They see it as irritating, frustrating, or bad, and wish it would go away— who wouldn't? But problems are more than unwanted troubles. They are opportunities to rise to a challenge, win a battle, and come out a superhero. Problems can turn you into a bold explorer. Problems make you wise. Never look at a problem and see just the problem. See the opportunities hiding behind it. Struggling to overcome that problem can make you strong. Finding a way around it will sharpen your smarts. Triumphing over it will make you an inspiration to others. Never let a problem defeat you. Instead, accept the challenge of a problem and jump into the whole, exciting experience.

> Problems are only opportunities in work clothes.
>
> Henry J. Kaiser

If you faint in the day of adversity, your strength is small.

Proverbs 24:10 AMP

A feeling of accomplishment always makes up for the work it required.

Make a habit of seeing a project through to the end, and you will always feel good about yourself.

Some undertakings can feel like climbing a mountain, can't they? You work and work and wonder if you'll ever reach the summit. Sometimes you have to go back and improve what you've already done. Sometimes you have to do that more than once. This is a lot of work, and some people might abandon a project or assignment, or they might only make a halfhearted effort, but not you. You appreciate the emotional rewards that come with giving your all. You understand that you can't plant your flag on the mountain's summit without climbing the mountain. Keep giving your all to everything you do. Don't give up. Persevere. You'll be glad you worked so hard when those personal rewards come and you can proudly say, "I did it!"

If I have ever made any valuable discoveries, it has been owing more to patient attention, than to any other talent.

Isaac Newton

You, take courage! Do not let your hands be weak, for your work shall be rewarded.

2 Chronicles 15:7 NRSV

Tomorrow's happiest memories can be the things you do with your family today.

The time you spend with your family is important to you, both for the present and the future.

Someday you may be surprised by which experiences turn out to be your fondest memories: the camping trip where all it did was rain, that seemingly never-ending car trip, and those embarrassing family pictures, jokes, and kisses from your mom and me. Oddly enough, the experiences that seem silly, embarrassing, or boring at the time often turn out to be the very experiences that draw you close to the important people in your life. The time you have with your family is a small part of your life span, but you'll benefit from the bonds you build during that time for the rest of your life. Today's experiences will be the memories that will someday make you smile. Save time for your family now. It's a good investment in your future.

No matter what you've done for yourself or for humanity, if you can't look back on having given love and attention to your own family, what have you really accomplished?

Lee Iacocca

To everything there is a season,
a time for every purpose under heaven.

Ecclesiastes 3:1 NKJV

*If you have fun playing the game,
it won't matter if you win or lose.*

*Focus on enjoying your leisure activities,
and you will increase both your happiness
and the happiness of those around you.*

Whether you're involved in a game or an athletic competition, always remember to keep appreciating the experience no matter what the outcome. The process is the major part of any game or leisure activity. Winning or losing is just that very small part that occurs at the end. And in the eternal scheme of things, it doesn't matter who wins or loses. As I know you know, getting upset or discouraged over something so small spoils the experience for both loser and winner, and that's no fun. You love to laugh, have a good time, and enjoy your friends; that's the true purpose of any leisure activity. Never take a game too seriously. Instead, keep your cheerful attitude. It will make the activity more fun for you and other players.

When the One Great Scorer comes to write against your name, He writes not that you won or lost—but how you played the game.

Grantland Rice

A cheerful heart is good medicine,
but a crushed spirit dries up the bones.

Proverbs 17:22 NIV

Life is more exciting when you're open to trying new things.

God makes all things new. Give Him the freedom to do it with every day of your life, and you will wind up with a life well worth living.

Life is one new experience after another. Every day is an open door for something unexpected, especially when you're young and just beginning your great adventure. Think of all the things waiting around the corner for you: new foods to try, new facts to learn, new sensations to experience, new places to see and people to meet, new skills to develop. Keep an open mind and be willing to try new things. (You may realize you actually like cauliflower!) Be open to new hobbies, interests, and opportunities. Allow God to take your life in unexpected directions. Never be afraid to step into uncharted territory, because that's where new discoveries are made. Be open to whatever exciting things God brings across your path.

Where there is an open mind there will always be a frontier.

Dorothea Brande

Be alert, be present. I'm about to do something brand-new. It's bursting out! Don't you see it? There it is! I'm making a road through the desert, rivers in the badlands.

Isaiah 43:19 MSG

Keep giving your all to everything you do.
Don't give up. Persevere.

Accept the challenge of a problem and
jump into the whole exciting experience.

You can reach your dreams if you make
your travel arrangements and then take
the necessary steps to get there.

Like a muscle, talent gets bigger the more you exercise it.

Develop your God-given talents, and He will find satisfying ways for you to use them.

God gives everyone talents. To some He gives the ability to assemble and fix things. To some He gives the ability to create music or stories out of thin air. To some He gives wisdom and great mental powers. To some He gives athletic talent, the ability to entertain, or the insight to negotiate peace. But those talents are a lot like muscles; they need to be used to grow. God wants you to enjoy the talents He's given you, and the only way to do that is to use them. Develop your unique gifts. Practice and strengthen them. Aim to make your talent as big as the Incredible Hulk's muscles. That way you'll be fit and ready to do all the great things God has in mind for you to do.

Use your gifts faithfully, and they shall be enlarged; practice what you know, and you shall attain to higher knowledge.

Matthew Arnold

Do not neglect the gift that is in you . . . Put these things into practice, devote yourself to them, so that all may see your progress.

1 Timothy 4:14–15 NRSV

You can share everything with God because He will listen to anything you have to say.

God cares about you and is interested in everything in your life.

There are some things you don't want to share with anyone. Some hopes may not seem possible; some hurts may run deep; some concerns may feel silly. You probably find yourself wishing you could talk with someone who would really understand and who wouldn't laugh. That's where God comes in. He will listen to everything you have to say. I can say this with confidence because He listens to me, too. He listens because He cares—more than your best friend, even more than your parents. He not only cares, but He has the wisdom you need and the power to enable you to work through your hardest problems. The next time you feel you're all alone or no one understands, don't despair. God is there. He's always ready to listen and to help.

> We should speak to God from our own hearts and talk to him as a child talks to his father.
>
> C. H. Spurgeon

Give all your worries and cares to God, for he cares about what happens to you.

1 Peter 5:7 NLT

The best way to appreciate your life is to think about all the good in it.

The more you focus on what's good in your life, the less you'll be able to see what's bad.

Everyone has Eeyore days once in a while—grumpy, blue days when the world seems to be spinning the wrong direction on purpose. But looking at life that way doesn't do a thing to make you feel better. And it sure doesn't make your life any better. So when those Eeyore days come, try taking a more positive look at your life. Remind yourself of the people who love you, that warm bed you sleep in, those free library books and DVDs you can check out any time you want. Think of the talents and hobbies you enjoy and all the body parts that work great. (Isn't it a cool thing to have taste buds?) When you really think about it, life is good. And my life is good because you're in it!

Keep your face to the sunshine, and you cannot see the shadows.

Helen Keller

Think about the things that are good and worthy of praise.
Think about the things that are true and honorable
and right and pure and beautiful and respected.

Philippians 4:8 NCV

"I'm sorry" are the two most powerful
words in the English language.

Never underestimate the
power of an apology.

Think of what those two small words—I'm sorry—can do. They can end quarrels, stop a fight before it begins, reunite friends, and make you feel like a new person. I remember telling a good friend I was sorry after I hurt her feelings, and it made a huge difference in how she felt about me. Say the words to your parents and mean them, and they can reduce a sentence of restriction for life down to something you can live with. Most important, they keep you humble and keep your heart in good emotional shape. Say them to the people in your life who deserve to hear them. You can even say them to people you think aren't so deserving, because when you do you will break down walls and build new beginnings. *I'm sorry* are two words you'll never regret saying.

A noble mind disdains not to repent.

Alexander Pope

If you enter your place of worship and, about to make an offering, you suddenly remember a grudge a friend has against you, abandon your offering, leave immediately, go to this friend and make things right.

Matthew 5:23–24 MSG

In all aspects of life, the most important person to compete against is yourself.

Instead of competing with others, concentrate on being your best self. You'll do fine.

We're a competitive society. Our sports are competitive, and our business environment is competitive. Even many of our TV shows involve competition, with people vying to see who can race around the world the fastest or survive on an island the longest. It's easy to think life is all about competing against others. But the most important person you have to best is yourself. Take the talents and gifts you've been given and grow them. Beat your own time. Work to learn more than you did last year. You don't need to be concerned with how your performance stacks up against some-one else's. Instead, just do your best to exceed your past performances. Play your own game well, and you'll eventually get your own unique reward from God.

> Doing your best is more important than being the best.
>
> Shannon Miller

I saw that all painful effort in labor and all skill in work comes from man's rivalry with his neighbor. This is also vanity, a vain striving after the wind and a feeding on it.

Ecclesiastes 4:4 AMP

*The best way to gain trust
is to show responsibility.*

*The secret to being trusted with more
freedom is to first prove yourself
trustworthy with responsibility.*

Here's a secret that will come in handy: the best way to get a later curfew, more privileges, or a more important position at work is to put the minds of those who are over you at ease. The more you prove that you're a responsible person, the more other people can and will trust you and the more privileges you'll earn. I'll bet you know kids who, the minute their parents' car leaves the driveway, say, "All right. Party on!" and then proceed to call fifty friends over and do just that. I know people who carry this kind of attitude into the work environment; they're slackers who let up the minute the boss's back is turned. Grandchild, continue to be your trustworthy self. It will earn you the trust of others. And that, in turn, will earn you much-deserved rewards.

> The price of greatness is responsibility.
>
> Winston Churchill

"Well done, my good servant!" his master replied.
"Because you have been trustworthy in a very
small matter, take charge of ten cities."

Luke 19:17 NIV

The way you win in life is by playing by God's rules.

God has established the rules for living a good life. Follow them, and you'll have good success.

Who doesn't want to do well in life? Everyone likes to come out a winner. Have you ever wondered why it is that some people live happy, winning lives while others seem to go from one mess to another? It all boils down to rules. Some people understand that life, like a good game, comes with a set of rules. Follow them and the game goes well. Break them and you suffer penalties. Since God made the rules, He obviously knows the best way to play the game. Following His rules guarantees you'll come out a winner. You already are a winner in my eyes. And I know you'll stay one because you're smart enough to get the connection between living by God's rules and having a winning life.

> Justice is the insurance we have on our lives, and obedience is the premium we pay for it.
>
> William Penn

Blessed (happy, fortunate, to be envied) is everyone who fears, reveres, and worships the Lord, who walks in His ways and lives according to His commandments.

Psalm 128:1 AMP

The next time you feel you're all
alone or no one understands,
don't despair. God is there.

God wants you to enjoy the talents
He's given you, and the only way
to do that is to use them.

When you really think about it,
life is good.

It's always wiser to talk to people than about people.

Never talk about another person unless you have something good to say.

Once in a while, friends can say or do things that frustrate you. There are bound to be times in your life when other people will hurt or disappoint you. When that happens, the best thing to do is to say how you feel, but say it calmly and gently. Try not to get upset, but simply talk to the person whose actions are bothering you. That can give the person a chance to explain or fix the problem—a much more effective method than simply pointing the finger at the other person's faults. It also gives you an opportunity to understand the other person. Some people will talk about a person's faults to everyone but that person, but that doesn't work. It's a lot more satisfying to be a problem-fixer and not a problem-maker.

> Do not listen gleefully to gossip at your neighbor's expense or chatter to anyone who likes finding fault.
>
> Saint Maximus the Confessor

If your fellow believer sins against you, go and tell him in private what he did wrong. If he listens to you, you have helped that person to be your brother or sister again.

Matthew 18:15 NCV

The way to keep friends is to look at your own faults and ignore theirs.

Accept your friends for who they are, and you'll all be happy.

Even though we all have faults, it's sometimes easier to see someone else's rather than our own. *Good grief. She always interrupts when I'm talking. Why does she always have to be the center of attention? He is the biggest ball hog on the court. I hate it when he . . . I hate it when she . . .* The funny thing is, we can be guilty of doing the very things that bug us in others. You can't change your friends' behavior. The only person you have any control over is yourself. Try not to be bothered by things your friends do that really don't make a difference. Overlook their flaws, and instead concentrate on eliminating yours—that's what I try to do. Your friends will appreciate the acceptance, and you'll benefit from the self-improvement.

> Bear with the faults of others as you would have them bear with yours.
>
> Phillips Brooks

Be completely humble and gentle; be patient,
bearing with one another in love.

Ephesians 4:2 NIV

*A failure is just a stubbed toe
on the road to success.*

*Learn from your failures, and then
move on. You have lots of great
adventures ahead of you.*

Failing can be painful, embarrassing, and frustrating, but it can be the first step to achievement. Failure is as much a part of life as success. In fact, failure is the secret ingredient that makes success so sweet when you finally get to taste it. Failure is how we learn what to do differently next time. Failure teaches us patience. It shows us where we need to improve and when we need to recruit help. One thing failure never does; failure never prevents anyone bent on success from achieving it. You don't let a subbed toe stop you from getting where you want to go. Never let a small thing like a failure stop you from completing the journey to reach your goals.

> Men's best successes come after their disappointments.
>
> Henry Ward Beecher

I consider that the sufferings of this present time are not worth comparing with the glory about to be revealed to us.

Romans 8:18 NRSV

It's always a good idea to let someone else do your bragging for you.

You'll always sound better when someone else sings your praises.

You're absolutely wonderful. I've known this for years. But you may want to get other people to recognize this fact, especially people you want to like you. One way is to keep doing good deeds and succeeding, and let someone else do your talking. Sooner or later someone will, you know. And that will be worth waiting for, because accomplishment somehow looks better when pointed to by a third party. The kind things you do have a way of not being so impressive when you tell about them yourself. Giving up bragging rights is called humility, and it's one of the rarest gifts of all. It's also one that people truly appreciate. Be humble. It can't hide how wonderful you are, but it will certainly enhance it.

The first test of a really great man is his humility.

John Ruskin

Don't praise yourself. Let someone else do it. Let the praise come from a stranger and not from your own mouth.

Proverbs 27:2 NCV

Follow the law, and you'll detour around a lot of trouble.

Make a lifetime habit of obeying the law, and trouble will have a much harder time finding you and those you care about.

You're smart enough to understand that real life doesn't work like the movies. Movie characters can plan elaborate heists and walk away with cool millions or can race hot cars all over town and avoid killing anyone. They break laws right and left and live happily ever after. But you know that in real life people break laws and live quite miserably. They get hauled off to jail. They get bad reputations that shadow them wherever they go. They get fines and humiliation, and they lose friends. Not cool. I learned it's a lot better to make a habit of keeping the law, even those seemingly small traffic laws. If you do that too, you'll spare both yourself and others. It's good that you understand that, no matter what anyone says, laws were not meant to be broken.

> Obedience to the law is demanded, not asked as a favor.
>
> Theodore Roosevelt

Remind the people to respect the government and be law-abiding, always ready to lend a helping hand.

Titus 3:1 MSG

You can always make a bad day better by doing something nice for someone else.

Helping other people will always make you feel better about who you are.

Doing something nice for someone else is like ice cream for your soul—it just makes you feel so good. That's because thinking about someone else, focusing on taking care of another person's needs, distracts you from your own problems. Making someone else smile makes you smile. You feel better about yourself, because having a positive impact on another person's life is like being God's hands on earth. Partnering with God—who wouldn't smile at getting an opportunity to do that? Next time you're in a slump, remember how good God has been to you, and pass it on. Look around and see whom you can help. Let your heart guide you and do something to make another person's day. You'll make your own in the process.

> A kind heart is a fountain of gladness, making everything in its vicinity freshen into smiles.
>
> Washington Irving

Be kind to one another, tenderhearted, forgiving one another, even as God in Christ forgave you.

Ephesians 4:32 NKJV

*Failure never prevents a person bent
on success from achieving it.*

*The only person you have any
control over is yourself.*

*The next time you're in a slump,
remember how good God has
been to you, and pass it on.*

Working together is the best way
to conquer big jobs.

Be willing to do your part of
the work, and you'll be able to
share in the rewards.

Cleaning the garage, moving, operating a company—some jobs are best done with more than one person. In fact, some jobs simply can't be done by one person. And some jobs aren't much fun to do alone. That's why it's important to go through life with a pitch-in-and-help attitude. When you work together with friends or family you can cut big jobs down to bite-size pieces. You can take on seemingly impossible challenges and accomplish great things. Whether it's cleaning the garage or building a house in a poor country, working with other people offers a sense of camaraderie and accomplishment and makes the work go faster. And that's a bonus, because the sooner the work gets done, the sooner everyone can have fun together.

> Teamwork divides the task and doubles the success.
>
> Author Unknown

We rebuilt the wall, and all the wall was joined together to half its height; for the people had a mind to work.

Nehemiah 4:6 NRSV

God is strong enough to carry you through any mess.

You'll be able to survive anything in life as long as you depend on God.

When that test is due tomorrow and you're not ready, whom do you turn to? When you've had a fight with your best friend and don't know how to fix it, what do you do? When you've done something you wish you hadn't and your life is a mess, what's your first reaction? Pray. When things look hopeless, when you're afraid, when your life gets out of control—those are the times God can pick you up and carry you through the mess. God has pulled me through many times when I've messed up. He made the world and everything in it, including you. Putting any broken pieces in your life back together isn't any harder for Him than it is for you to gather up your dirty clothes. So whenever you have trouble, remember you also have God.

> He rides at ease whom the grace of God carries.
>
> Thomas à Kempis

The name of the LORD is a strong tower;
the righteous run to it and are safe.

Proverbs 18:10 NIV

Leave your hurts in the past so that your present and future can be better.

Enjoy and appreciate what you have now, and plan for your future. Leave the past behind you, where it belongs.

It's no fun to get hurt, is it? People can say and do things to you that make you feel really bad. It can be hard to get over those hurts, but it's worse to hang on to them. Going over and over the unkind things people have done to you, thinking continually about how wrong and unfair they were, is like leaving a bee's stinger in your skin. The hurt won't stop. Always pull out those hurts. Ask God to help you forgive and to redirect your focus in a new and better direction. Quit looking back to where you've been, and concentrate instead on where you're going. If you do that, your present will be happier and you'll build yourself a better future.

> If you hug to yourself any resentment against anybody else, you destroy the bridge by which God would come to you.
>
> Peter Marshall

Don't get me wrong: By no means do I count myself an expert in all of this, but I've got my eye on the goal, where God is beckoning us onward—to Jesus. I'm off and running, and I'm not turning back.

Philippians 3:13–14 MSG

What you do with the money you have is what makes you rich.

Invest in the things that really count in life, and your life will be good.

Did you know you have the potential to be really, really rich? No, I'm not talking about money. That's just a tool. I'm talking about your life. You have the capacity to enjoy a rich life no matter how much money you ever get your hands on. If you spend your money on good things like good books and music, an education, or your friends, you can't help but have a life that's rich in wisdom, enjoyment, and lasting friendships. If you invest in a good education, a good home, and a good cause, you'll have a life rich in purpose. Many of the most important investments don't require a fortune, but what you get for your money will make you richer than most millionaires.

> Make no mistake, my friend, it takes more than money to make men rich.
>
> A. P. Gouthey

Jesus said to him, "If you want to be perfect,
go, sell what you have and give to the poor,
and you will have treasure in heaven;
and come, follow Me."

Matthew 19:21 NKJV

*The secret to succeeding
is to keep trying.*

*You have a better chance of getting
the things you really want in life
if you don't give up trying.*

Some things don't happen the first time we try them: a perfect hoop shot, playing a Chopin sonata with no mistakes, mastering a difficult math concept. In fact, most things worth having or doing require practice and continued effort. The good news is that the more you try, the better you get and the greater your chances of success. The more shots you take, the closer you are to making a basket. The more jobs you check out, the closer you get to finding the right one for you. Always keep trying, because that is what helps you improve and that is what takes you closer to your goal. Some people give up, never realizing how close they were to succeeding. I know you won't be one of them.

Persistent people begin their success where others end in failure.

Edward Eggleston

If you faint in the day of adversity, your strength is small.

Proverbs 24:10 NKJV

*The best advice always comes from
the people who care the most.*

*Trust the people who love you—their
only agenda is your well-being.*

No one knows it all. Everyone needs help and can learn from others. That's why advice is important. As you go through life, you'll find that everyone has some for you. You probably already get a lot of advice (especially from your parents and a certain grandparent). When you're sorting through all that advice, remember that the best council is most likely to come from those who love you the most. Friends often have a hidden agenda. They want you to do what is good for them. Many experts also have an agenda. They want to sell you their services. But the people who really love you want you to succeed. Always remember, when someone who cares gives you advice, listen. It's going to be good.

He that is taught only by himself has a fool for a master.

Ben Johnson

My child, listen to your father's teaching
and do not forget your mother's advice.

Proverbs 1:8 NCV

Quit looking back to where you've been,
and concentrate instead on
where you're going.

You have the capacity to enjoy a rich
life no matter how much money
you ever get your hands on.

The more you try, the better you get and
the greater your chances of success.

Wise choices make for good living.

*Making wise choices guarantees
a better life.*

With all you have going for you, I expect your life to be full of good things. One way you can ensure that happening is to think of your life as an adventure story you write yourself, with each choice bringing something new into it. And the better your choices, the better the adventure. Make smart food choices, and you'll have health and energy for all kinds of fun physical activities. Make good moral choices, and you'll sidestep a huge pile of unhappiness. Pick interesting hobbies, and you'll find satisfaction. Choose to get up and not let yourself be a couch potato, and you'll live life instead of watching it. I can hardly wait to see all the great adventures you'll have because of the smart choices you make.

In the long run, we shape our lives and we shape ourselves. The process never ends until we die, and the choices we make are ultimately our responsibility.

Eleanor Roosevelt

Dear friend, guard Clear Thinking and Common Sense with your life; don't for a minute lose sight of them. They'll keep your soul alive and well, they'll keep you fit and attractive. You'll travel safely, you'll neither tire nor trip.

Proverbs 3:21–23 MSG

Helping someone in need is like giving a gift to God.

When you help others, you make their lives better, and you make your heavenly Dad proud.

Have you ever thought that when you loan someone lunch money or help a friend study for a test you're giving a gift to God? You are, because when you do a kindness to one of God's children you do a kindness to Him. When you help someone created in His image, it's as if you give God a bouquet of heavenly roses. Doing what your heavenly Father wants you to do encourages Him, and, as your parents can tell you, that is always the best gift of all. Keep giving to God by giving to His kids. Put money in the offering at church, help the needy, visit the elderly, share your skills and resources. Be generous, and you'll find you can't outgive God.

Those who bring sunshine into the lives of others cannot keep it from themselves.

James M. Barrie

He who has pity on the poor lends to the Lord,
and that which he has given He will repay to him.

Proverbs 19:17 AMP

The biggest thrills are the ones that build character.

Spend time on activities that will make you a better person.

Life is exciting. It's full of places to go, sights to see, and things to do. You've tried your hand at many things already, and you'll enjoy trying lots more things in your life. Some of them—like catching a lightning bug and then letting it fly away unharmed—are small but exciting. But the big thrills come from smart living and achievement. Cheers from a crowd as you make a rebound, take a bow onstage, or race to the finish line are exhilarating, but they're not as important as the accomplishment itself. With accomplishment you have the lasting satisfaction of personal growth. You deserve the best in life, and I know you'll get it when you live in a smart way.

Adventure is not outside a man; it is within.

David Grayson

Run away from infantile indulgence. Run after mature righteousness—faith, love, peace—joining those who are in honest and serious prayer before God.

2 Timothy 2:22 MSG

Before you do anything, always remind yourself that God sees everything.

Staying aware of the fact that God is always with you will help you stay clear of a lot of wrong behavior.

Somebody is always looking. God. One really great way to make sure you stay on track is by remembering that God is your constant companion and friend. God is with you, and He sees you always. Walk hand in hand with God, and He'll help you avoid doing things you may regret later. Some of the most dangerous moments are those times when you're all alone. Those are the times when bad advice whispers, "Go ahead. No one will know." Those are the times when it's easy to make a misstep. Just remember that God is with you always, and let your actions please Him. Ask yourself, *Do I really want God to see me doing this?* If the answer is no, then you'll know what to do.

Character is what you are in the dark.

Dwight L. Moody

You know when I sit down and when I rise up;
you discern my thoughts from far away.

Psalm 139:2 NRSV

One of the most important things you can give God is your youth.

Let God work in your life now, while you're young, and you'll reap the benefits for a lifetime.

Have you ever thought about how valuable you are to God? You are an exciting bundle of enthusiasm and new ideas. You have health and an energy level your grandparents can only remember. You have the strength and the years ahead of you to do all kinds of wonderful things. What a great time to commit yourself to living for God. Giving God your youth gets you started in life on the right foot. You make wise choices, which make for a good future. Using your fresh outlook and energy, God can make things happen. Of course, every phase of your life will bring its own unique rewards, but there's no time quite as potential-packed as your youth. Give it to God, and you won't be sorry.

Those who are wholly God's are always happy.

François Fénelon

Don't let the excitement of youth cause you to forget your Creator. Honor him in your youth before you grow old and no longer enjoy living.

Ecclesiastes 12:1 NLT

Be a lifelong learner, and your life will always be interesting.

Learning during your school years is important; learning during your lifetime is exciting.

Do you remember when you were little and first learning to read? How excited you'd get when you saw a word you knew or when you could open a book and string together a whole sentence of words? You don't ever have to lose that sense of excitement because, as you go through life, you'll find there is always something new to learn, some new discovery waiting for you around the next corner. Think of the places you can go and the experiences you can collect. Think of all the hobbies you can try and the skills you can master. The people who lead the most interesting lives treat the world as their schoolroom. I know you'll want to be one of them.

Anyone who stops learning is old, whether twenty or eighty. Anyone who keeps learning stays young.

Henry Ford

Happy (blessed, fortunate, enviable) is the man who finds skillful and godly Wisdom, and the man who gets understanding [drawing it forth from God's Word and life's experiences].

Proverbs 3:13 AMP

God is the world's best guidance counselor, so trust Him to guide your life.

God wants and knows what's best for you. You can trust Him with your life.

Trying to decide what to do with the rest of your life can feel overwhelming. What direction should you go? What talents should you develop? What interests should you pursue? Guidance counselors can help, but they may not always know best. How can they when they don't know your hidden talents or your secret dreams and hopes? Test scores don't tell everything, and what they do tell isn't always an accurate future predictor. There is One who knows you intimately, who realizes your worth and your potential and who knows the perfect path for your life: God. Don't be afraid to walk through the doors He opens. Don't be afraid to open any opportunity He sends your way. He'll guide you well.

> God always gives His very best to those who leave the choice to Him.
>
> James Hudson Taylor

In all your ways acknowledge Him, and He shall direct your paths.

Proverbs 3:6 NKJV

The people who lead the most interesting lives treat the world as their schoolroom.

You'll want to invest your life in the big thrills that come from smart living and achievement.

The better your choices, the better the adventure.

He rides at ease whom the grace of God carries.

Thomas à Kempis

The name of the LORD is a strong tower;
the righteous run to it and are safe.

Proverbs 18:10 NIV